MANHATTAN

Erik Pihel

Palamedes
San Francisco

Copyright © 2015 by Erik Pihel
All Rights Reserved

Palamedes Publishing
www.palamedes.pub
San Francisco

Cover by Kate Marchio
www.katemarchiophotography.com

ISBN 978-0-692-36791-9
Printed in the United States of America

Also available in ebook:
Kindle 726e467a-919f-448b-8601-c07f18db5e09
EPUB 0fc6784a-1e0c-4555-93e4-0c8f2c158455
www.palamedes.pub/books/manhattan

LCCN 2015905616

www.facebook.com/PalamedesPub
www.twitter.com/PalamedesPub

Saturday, 9 December 1995   1

1 The World Below   2
2 The Passion of the Queen   8
3 A Bridge to the Far Shore   13
4 The Immigrants Embark   21

Friday, 5 July 1996   31

5 Stranger at the Gates   32
6 Battle at the Wall   39
7 Shape Shifter   47

Saturday, 6 July 1996   61

8 Flight from the City   62
9 The Immigrants Arrive   69

Sunday, 7 July 1996   76

10 One More Strange Island   77

Appendix: New Yorkers in "The Immigrants Embark" 91
Acknowledgements 102
About the Author 103

SATURDAY, 9 DECEMBER 1995

1 The World Below

I

I walked past street cops, magazine stops, City Light
and Earth First T-shirt shops, red meters, sign-
readers,
trash cans stashed with sucked-out umbrellas, coverless fuck
　　books, and torn bus maps—voices smoked the cold
toward blinking DONT WALK that froze
into steady light—walked into the stampede
under gaudy, flash-green lights, and street theater
where icy sidewalk was a wet tongue licking soles
of countless feet—42nd Street waiting to fold
me into its mouth: a mouth that can't breathe,
can't taste, can't kiss, and can't sing—can only devour
and digest, compress and arrest me in the barrage of torn-up
　　tar
holes, car horns, porn wars, and worn-out radio dials—
　　sounds
growing down into the underground through streets and up
　　towers
teach me to listen and start in the heart
of the grid *in medias res, in medias* town.

The morning music danced down the avenue, spinning
   around
sounds of a city riddled with glitter
and I arrived from out of town into the grid
of the world, offered change to a vanishing cup amid
wounded asking for help, homeless laying in dirt,
found a staircase down, and descended into the Earth.

II

　　Outside the gates, the ferryman ignored
me. I leaned into the glass and said, "One."
Unfazed by the street souls descending toward
　　him, Times Square's guardian sat before tunnels
and pushed a token under glass. I clicked
through stiles to the 1/9. A crowd came running
　　to the banks—they leaned over tracks, checked ticking
wall-clocks, and dreamed of worlds above, of fleeing
the mazes to towers of golden brick,
　　far from these disordered caves. I walked seeing
our last moments, the book bags, the arranged
car idling—we stood under changing trees
　　on that October day, already strangers.
I took quick looks at your face; silhouetted
on sidewalk, you explained the stock exchange—
　　I nodded. A bus roared. I said Annette,
but your name was lost in the street noise, freed
by the traffic, and slipped away on metal
　　and wheels. We stood still in the falling leaves
and you pulled back into your silent spaces.
I didn't know what to say. So don't be
　　a stranger, you said, and left our last place
without turning. You opened a door, Brooklyn-

bound, and vanished in the glare, leaving traces
    of glass and metal. 1/9's ceiling shook;
I walked one flight down to 7, already
full, where the Queens-bound leaned over tracks, looking
    for a headlight in darkness. If I'd said
don't go, you might have turned back, our bridge tottering
in the wind, but supports collapsed instead,
    and I stopped as the bridge fell into water.
A train roared through my head; the platform cleared.
I needed to be bored. I walked past nodders
    on headphones and climbed to 1/9. Still peering
down trainless tracks, travelers checked wrists, retraced
their steps. A rumbling—some covered their ears;
    some lifted startled babies or briefcases
to see lights take them to expensive cliffs—
darkness. The rumbling was elsewhere. They paced,
    re-checked wrists, and exhaled, a growing rift
with the cavern whose mazes for un-noted
ages were solid schist: the hieroglyphic
    rock of Manhattan, unmoved by exploding
dynamite or, at the slightest touch, splitting
in thin leaves. The island's deeper abodes
    remained dormant, the undiscovered city
below the city and what slept in rock:
signal lights, phone lines, water pipes to kitchens—

    connections were missing—til men unlocked
shacks stacked with dynamite sticks they could fix
into dark spaces—then explosions shocked
    the ancient stone, leaving a dried-out Styx
with hollow depths and lonely places, trackless
and silent. Some rushed for exits. Some quick
    clicked down staircases. No train. Travelers tackled
turnstiles, looked for stairs. The wound had no doors—
I descended ramps to N/R, news-stacks
    in strange language, map-readers of Astoria's
yellow lines. The wound had outgrown its clothes—
if I'd said: the night we ran on the shore,
    remember talks in cafés, walks through snow-
covered trails, but I kept these til my head
was a haunted attic—I did not know
    death would feel so strong. Rows of cracked lights led
us through tunnels. Don't be a stranger, you
said, and walked without looking back—you'd read
    your *Orpheus* and your *Exodus* too—
or was it your *Genesis*—and collapsing
bridges had sent you to shores of the new,
    while I'd arrived where the lost have read maps
since nineteen four when these tunnels were blasted:
the birth of Times Square, burning steamship trapped
    at Hell Gate, and seekers who spent their last

moments unaware as they walked new rails,
dawdling in the lights, that subways were faster
    than horses. The A rumbled through the trail
of New York disasters. I stepped in, stared
at ads for design school and learning Braille,
    transferred, and rode an L to Union Square.
Doors slid apart. We walked worn ground and crossed
the gates, herding to a staircase. Cold air
    blew from the world above; I looked up, lost
my step in stampede of ascending feet
on wet steps, then emerged, awake, exhausted,
    into the snowfall on East 14th Street.

2 The Passion of the Queen

I walked through this world in flakes descending
    to Earth as beeping plows scraped street, wheels smeared
    snow. I turned onto 7th to meet Jennifer
    and monks at 𝔅𝔲𝔯𝔭 𝔒𝔞𝔰𝔱𝔩𝔢: 𝔗𝔢𝔪𝔭𝔩𝔢 𝔬𝔣 𝔅𝔢𝔢𝔯
    𝔚𝔬𝔯𝔰𝔥𝔦𝔭. Whenever we pilgrimaged here
    to the temple, Jennifer would insist
    on her Arthurian name Guenivere—
    I related the howling storm that hist
my heart and she told tales of Lancelots she'd kissed.

Medieval walls bounded us, drawn with drunk
    scribes writing scrolls with "a wise man has built
    his house on the rock," while Franciscan monks
    walked castle floors, lit candles, and wiped spilt
    beer from tables. Guenivere's story-quilt
    of sailors on the whale-road and their linkings
    filled the hall. The mead cups balanced on tilting
    tables and we swallowed the spirits, sinking
into the calming waters of Lethean drink.

Then down to a lair where a Dragon caught
    in ice roared at separation, its rude,
    flapping wing-wind freezing the cellar taut
    round its entrapt, scaly flesh as it chewed
    an empty mouth, dreaming me into food
    for its rumbling pangs. I pointed my lance
    straight at the wall-building fiend Solitude,
    for needs must slay it before I could dance
drunkenly to the friars' Gregorian chants.

The fair queen Guenivere reversed her foamy
    spirit-cup and sang melody unplanned:
    the mead-hall rang with roundly voice that roamed
    the ranges famous for a wand'ring band
    of rogues and knaves known in these rocky lands
    as Pearl Jam. The Keeper of the Cell heard
    this musick wylder than woodgods and handed
    Guenivere a redipped chalice. "Your words
and that…voice," he mused. "I'm Fradubio the Third."

Fradubio espied the goodly lady
    in smart snow boots yclad; faces they wore
    changed into masks for the ancient charade.
    He released the tap and caught the downpour
    in frosted glass, then thus bespake: "I've storied
    with many a mouth—traders of gold, flyers
    of the eagle-roads—but ne'er heretofore
    has such light lit castle halls; the reply
in thine eyes makes this merry monk curse God's sunrise."

I saw in temple walls the snake-like arc
    of bygone suitors, the roomeful of men
    that haunted Guenivere's strange dreams: Sir Mark
    of Jersey, worthy squire who e'er extendeth
    whistles to ladykind; Sir Thom of Greenwich,
    stumbler toward the Grete See; Sir Michael, next
    in the cycle, Duke of Vlachte Bos, pen
    pusher, and, one night's excess be told, wrecker
of mead-benches; Alex of Chelsea, scribe of texts

holy and worldly; Sir David, wheel-guider
    along the Heere Wegh and York's rush-hour mazes;
    Sir Brian of Breuckelen, an outridere
    and ziekentrooster, healing with kind phrases.
    I watched the order recede into haze,

fading through our Guenivere's busy years.
"But we two could spark this citie ablaze,"
whispered Fradubio, and Guenivere
returned a wide smile that was neither now nor here.

Solitude woke with a whip of spiked tail;
    stony flesh scraped the chamber's icy floors,
    clanging broken swords and rusted chain-mail,
    and I walked the shores of an ancient war,
    candle-flames dancing in Solitude's roar,
    fighting arrows and dots painted on charts
    of mine own making, and I could no more:
    I turned the lance to attack mine own heart,
cornered in private borough of internal art.

Guenivere, sad to see my darkened face,
    cride out, "Now now, sir knight, shew what ye bee,
    add sight to your might and turn toward a place
    that outgroweth the tale of mine and mee."
    She shewed mee the door for mine eyes to see;
    inside was a citie shimmering bright:
    metal Tigers with eye-lights roaring free
    and square-headed Giants standing to heights
of the starry sphere, glistred in glorious Light.

Solitude roared and I, whelmd from ygoe,
    looked down the rocky path of 7th Street;
    beside a fire hydrant dusted with snow,
    I stayed the step to bid farewell. My feet
    fell in 3rd Ave's rhythms, caught the downbeat
    of passing cars—a swarm of brakelights traced
    across shop windows, streaking the concrete.
    My head ached from too many thoughts; I chased
them away and caught a subway at Astor Place.

3 A Bridge to the Far Shore

The downtown 6 train rattled toward the river.
The Unseen Voice made sounds in crackling speakers.
Nobody moved. Dark windows mirrored slivers

of light. Didn't know what to say. Nine weeks
since Annette left, my head ached from the beer
and blizzard, and how things had gotten. "Bleecker

Street. Change here for B, D, Q, F. Stand clear
of the closing doors." Nobody changed. Doors
closed. I wanted to say something. Change here

for language trains. We rumbled toward the shore.
"Spring Street," the Unseen Voice said. "Downtown local."
I sat in my borough of local stories,

folded notes, old photos, a chain of broken
bridges, as if the only isle I'd known
was my own. "Brooklyn Bridge is next and final."

Don't be a stranger, you said, crossed another
city's gates, mad birds circling, and I wandered
aisles, staying clear of the closing doors. One

more train arrived. "All exit," said the Voice.
Emerged from the tunnel, bridge tower poised
at the beginning of the world. I searched

for a city, the noise of all past Troys
silent as a boneyard under fogged arches.
Turned from the wind, walked backwards into mist,

the road ahead slipping away in history's
ink-stained planks, blurred lanes, a bottomless river,
waves of forgotten rhythms, word graves, sound

caves, chained voices waiting for a breath-giver—
bring the stones for the language bridge. The wounded
walk this bridge, healed, to a city whose music

retunes and changes, a temple for moon
gods, a lover of strangers—I back-tracked
near the lost city somewhere in the snow.

I couldn't see what was there, and instead
saw shadows arrive from the underground:
Lenape walking uptown trail grids, paddling

tree-trunk boats upriver; traders downtown
hiding traps in forests of Manahatta;
couples cracking stalks in Gowanus Creek

maize fields. I watched the ancient figures matter
of factly go about their business, speaking
new words in unfamiliar land. Somewhere

in hidden lights of the Brooklyn Inn, breathing
smoky air, Annette drank from taps of Lethe
that sew forgetfulness and free from care.

Your naked face opened like an airhole—
I walked up close and inhaled the first breath
of death: it smelled like peppermint. Unfold

me, I said, and your hands slid through my deaths,
winds became irrelevant, and night lightly
tapped its tambourine through the moonlit halls.

A door opened in the middle of night.
When new light dawned on the world and its walls,
this land was unbroken, wild, and unseen

until glacier carved a river between
Manahatta and Seawanhaka. Streaming
through the new in-betweens, the river wailing,

your wet eyes shimmered like a see-through dress
until I saw your head was full of nails—
then you closed the door; I made myself less.

Once, long ago, a moving ice sheet scattered
this place, ripping off rock chunks; scraped and flattened
Earth to raw roots; scooped out valleys. The battered

bedrock bore the weight. Arctic angels fanned
the surface with wing-gusts, freezing the land
in Eternity. Then the world began

to melt. Cave-roofs dripped water-sticks. Ground shattered
and splintered in ice-lightning. Solid matter
dissolved. Tops of white mountains broke—long shadows

tilting—then the ripped rock roared down and vanished
into the white Earth. Pines and birches branded
thawing tundra, the melting overran

valleys with rushing rivers, and a mandolin
in the primordial waters—Manhattan
Island—opened its scarred face to the skies—

I turned back toward Breuckelen, broken land,
razed by the same sheet that left sloping high
solitude. A bridge maker came to heal

the wound. He raised towers that drew the sky
line's first outlines and became urns for holed
workers who burned in the chambers—the steel

cables held despite the traders who sold
untested wire, and a book closed unread,
a door opened, and don't leave or the side

walks will echo your name and things we said
will be lies and don't leave unless you're sure
and please don't leave until my wet feet find

flowering grip tape on the bathtub floor
and don't leave when the fabric of our blinds
is still unrolling and the coastline's seas

are flooding and until I find my charted
maps please don't leave and don't leave when the tree
that's still growing pushes roots through my heart

and don't leave unless my heart is a swinging
curtain and you need to walk in the sand
and don't leave til I've written everything

down and now, now is not a good time and
don't leave until the song ends and the road
and the world is a cold place without you—

grunting horses galloped their bundled loads
toward the pier, pulling creaking wagons through
December fog and, as the clopping drove

coachmen to the ferry docks, no one knew
how much bad wire had been forever woven
into the cables. The builder spent days

paralyzed in his prison watching workers
suspended high above the water raise
towers and sink caissons. I overheard

New York's opening cheers for the next phase
of the city. They heard speeches of unions,
crossroads, breaking dawns, but their faith in New

York was not strong enough—and when someone
yelled, "The bridge is falling!," the awful rush
began. Those swept up in the herd tried jumping

to the river, but, no room to climb, crushed
friends against railings, lost their hats, and thumped
faces into the path. The bridge absorbed

the stampede, steel knots swaying in the roar,
towers unmoved. Runners reached shore and looked
back, stunned to see the bridge standing. Survivors

waited for horse carriages to arrive
with help. Manhattan stared at Brooklyn. Brooklyn
stared back at Manhattan. The blood-stained planks

stretched across the sparkling waters between
them. Few moved from the safety of the banks
to find breathing somewhere above the green

water, a woman screaming to Lord God
to help her husband off the wooden slats—
then clopping horses arrived, and the bodies

of the dead were carried to Manhattan.

4 The Immigrants Embark

I

From the ancient bridge,[1] I looked toward the city,[2]
the little graveyard where my people are,[3]
and heard the mermaids singing[4]
that cry that has rung through the ages,[5]
written on the subway walls[6] and immortal pages:[7]
whoever has suffered much and wandered much[8]
fain wad lie down.[9]

I too walk'd the streets of Manhattan island[10]
past garbage cans chained to concrete anchors;
walked under black painted fire escapes,[11]
the down-town streets, the jobbers' houses of business.[12]
I too felt the curious abrupt questionings stir within me[13]
from going to and fro in the Earth,
and from walking up and down in it.[14]

I saw flashing lights of surpassing brightness,[15]
and further still at an unearthly height,[16]
live from New York, it's Saturday night.[17]
I have outwalked the furthest city light[18]
and this also has been one of the dark places.[19]

Now more than ever seems it rich to die,
to cease upon the midnight with no pain.[20]
I have gone at dusk through narrow streets.[21]
I have looked down the saddest city lane.[22]
Manhattan's streets I saunter'd pondering[23]
when I felt a Funeral, in my Brain,
and Mourners to and fro kept treading down[24]
my chamber door[25] til I going in seine[26]
rolling on the river[27] older than
the flow of human blood in human veins[28]
and I can no more;[29] mother, mak my bed
soon, for I'm sick at the heart, and I fain
wad lie down.[30] The internal wound bleeds on
in silence.[31] Doctor, let me die.[32] Unchain
my heart.[33] Let the boys bring flowers in last month's
newspapers[34] and the smalle raine downe can raine—[35]
Christ you know it ain't easy that my love[36]
were in my armes, and I in my bed againe.[37]

II

What am I saying?[38] Where am I?[39]
What madness changes me out of myself?[40]
I have sat and listened to too many words,[41]
heard what the talkers were talking[42]
upon a hundred thousand stages[43]
and in the maker's rage to order words[44]
had become death, destroyer of[45] the sound I love,
the sound of the human voice.[46]

Poets come in the evening into the Old City:[47]
saints and poets and world-redeemers,[48]
English poets who grew up on Greek.[49]
The great Walt[50] is inside the wall.[51]
Coleridge stands[52] among the radiant stars.[53]
Robert Frost at midnight[54] sings hymns at heaven's gate.[55]
The city was filled with the crowd[56]
and the gates of this Chapel were shut.[57]
High piled books[58] are full, full of wise voices[59]
that little room is left for any more[60]
for It is always what It was before—[61]
Homer, the sovereign poet,[62]
Sapphò, the lyric poetess,[63]
clerics and popes and cardinals,[64]

and everybody wants to be special here—[65]
Emily Dickinson's horses,[66]
that funny money-man,[67]
four lads who shook the world.[68]

I am not Aeneas, I am not Paul.[69]
No! I am not Prince Hamlet,[70]
but a stranger and a wanderer[71] in eternal exile[72]
standing in the middle of nowhere[73] outside city and wall—[74]
my name was not found written in the book of life—[75]
I am nobody;[76] I'm Nobody;[77] my name is Nobody,[78]
deprived of heaven for no fault other than my lack of faith.[79]

This I murmured in my sleepe[80]
when rivers ancient as the world[81]
became a man and sent a voice from the deep eddy:[82]
    Come, let's build a city from the beginning.[83]
    To create a city,[84] you must change your home,[85]
    stand at the crossroads[86] and hear all sounds running
        together.[87]
    Within the fires are the spirits[88]
    and all will be changed, in a moment, in the glance of an
        eye.[89]
    Awake now, stranger, and come to the city.[90]
    Come build in the empty house of the stare.[91]

He spoke, burning with fire, and his clear current seethed,[92]
but I, knowing only a part,[93]
heard the sound of horns and motors.[94]

III
Let us go then, you and I,[95]
where old gods lie buried,[96]
where the underworld can meet the elite,[97]
and gather all the talk[98]
in a web of fabulous grass and eternal voices[99]
and build our bridge across it,[100]
make it up as we go along[101]
to the turning into yesterday's street,[102]
the gathering in New York.[103]

This place is just a shell,[104]
I heard a voice whisper—the authoritative voice—[105]
there is nothing here to see.[106]
But how shall I...make me room there: reach me a...[107]
Keep it down now,[108] the Voice said,[109]
blaspheming against the Holy Breath,[110]
the origin of all poems.[111]
Answer me to what I ask you.[112]

Is there anything you hold sacred in this world?[113]
Streets and lanes.[114] Faces and eyes.[115] Human voices.[116]
Shall we forsake our gods for a mad poet?[117]
The gods have changed[118] into the streets of the world.[119]

But who would count Eternity in[120] *howling at crossroads?*[121]
Lift up your eyes[122] in the city of nine doors.[123]
Have you the key? a voice asked.[124]
To articulate sweet sounds together is to work.[125]
Where are the crosses?[126]
On the sidewalks of New York.[127]

You answer well, said the invisible voice,[128]
but here there is no light.[129]
These city walls are like a prison.[130]

But look, what lights come yond?[131]
A city in my mind,[132] its hour come round at last.[133]
What city?[134] *What is the night?*[135] *What is Truth?*[136]
Worlds disappear, gods disappear, scriptures disappear[137]
into the secret house of death[138]
and the nothing that is[139]
on the outlying coasts beyond the whale-road[140]
that beats upon the high shore of this world.[141]
Which shore? Which shore?[142]
There is no shore, so these ripples will go on,[143]
turning and turning in the widening gyre,[144]
and before I built a wall I'd ask to know[145]
how far the ripples of our decisions go.[146]
But how shall I[147] *drive our ships to new land,*[148]

27

a port city on the shore of eternity?[149]
There is no port[150] and roads go ever ever on,[151]
all goes onward and outward[152]
and precipices show untrodden green.[153]
Should I, after tea and cakes and ices,[154]
wait around for that story to unfold?[155]
Here's where the story ends,[156]
proclaimed at market crosses, read in churches.[157]
Stories morph and reappear[158] in new sockets,[159]
shattered into hundreds of separate links[160]
till the bridge you will need be form'd.[161]

Whatcha gonna do, about it??[162]
change. change.[163]

IV

I've read the words[164] of all my buried ancestors[165]
and being but a broken man,[166] a broken voice,[167]
break up their lines[168]
and madly play with my forefathers' joints,[169]
later words first, first words last,[170]
mixing everything up,[171]
playing tennis without a net,[172]
working, yet not taking credit,[173]
the words of my book nothing, the drift of it every thing—[174]

I saw the holy city[175]
and I was a stranger and you invited me in[176]
to glue it back together,[177]
the previous order of the words[178]
broken off so that I could be grafted in[179]
the ancient bridge[180]
def with the record that was mixed a long time ago—[181]
patterns engraved, not so easily erased,[182]
my real voice is further further down, in another place—[183]

I was plural,[184] a scroll-swallower,[185]
stranger of here and everywhere,[186]
a book separate, not link'd with the rest,[187]

an extremely strange listener[188] who listens in the snow—[189]
hello emptiness,[190] I am nobody,[191]
and you were meant for me and I was meant for you.[192]

The Earth opened its mouth[193]
and out of that silence came thousands of voices—[194]
all the world's sounds began again,[195]
voice by voice,[196]
flames begotten of flame,[197] fire is their home,[198]
burning in spirit,[199] the smoke of my own breath,[200]
and all these explosions have been blessed—[201]

at this the door bolts automatically gave way,[202]
the gate to all mystery[203] springing back at the swift song,[204]
and I woke up in New York City,[205]
stepped over the threshold,[206]
and started walking home across the Bridge.[207]

Friday, 5 July 1996

5 Stranger at the Gates

I

Walked past honking trucks at the tunnel entrance,
lined like huge turtles crawling toward descent
into the river. Walked past yesterday's
parties, 9th Ave lined with holiday maze:
burnt strands, torn masks, shattered fire crackers, rotting
peels—trash cans stashed with sparklers, empty bottles,
folded news. Walked uptown past yesterday's
churches, boarded doors; stopped by traffic, waited
at crossroads for lights. Idling Porsches growled
like caged animals awaiting a prowl—
lights changed and they screamed off. Stopped at a gate
with a sign, "Open House at 10," a straight
path home along the less-expensive edges
of a city of golden roofs and ledges
with silver gargoyles. Walked up steps and joined
the line. We invaded the house and pointed
at furniture, entered living room doors,
and filled out forms when someone said, "There's four
gazillion people here; no way we're getting
this place." Left forms on the stove's blackened metal—
walked through someone else's kitchen, retreated
down the staircase, and returned to the street.

II

Golden brick blinded me, heard what was spoken
Inside the canyon walls, stuttered in broken
Voices on 42nd's stripe across
Earth. Thundering feet fell in sync, formed hostile

Lines of soldiers for a moment, then scattered
Over Times Square like a tap dance gone mad,
Vectors moving under tickers that cast
Everything in pixelated light: ...MASS

GRAVES BOSNIA...COMIC-CON STARTS...LAND MINES
IGNITE OUTRAGE...A'S CLIP ANGELS...mute lines
Vanished around the corner as if chasing
Electricity back, back to the flame

Lamps of the first city, Ur, a fire-lit
Outland between the rivers where scribes witnessed
Visions of sign-grids and into wet clay
Etched arrows, crosses, and circles of traded

Goods that kilns baked into books, recorded
In silence Moon Day morning's ox-swaps, stored
Voiceless sounds, unaware what they'd begun
Engraving those slabs drying in the sun:

Lights shifting, spiralling into word-bands
Overwhelmed my eyes. Looked back to news-stand
Vendors on the street, crossed Broadway, 6th, train
Entrances, and walked over bolted drain

Grates past Bryant Park's subways, crowds descending
Into the Earth to change places again,
Violinist sawing Bach into traffic,
Echoed street sounds, mirrored glass, rising scaffolds,

Long hair braided with bells that rang the rhythm
Of a woman walking through sun-shimmered
Vapor. She reached stairs and, turning to go,
Escaped with a bored sigh to shades below.

III

I stopped at 5th Avenue that divides
east and west, the passage where worlds collide
and shift order. Turned north along the border
and walked through the corridor past shoe stores,
Chase Manhattan Bank, metal floor-doors—"Active
Basement Keep Clear." Crossed 53rd to cracked
stones at Saint Thomas Church. "Change for the strange.
Change for the insane. Change for the deranged."
A man sat on the stone steps under
> COME IN PRAY
> FOR PEACE
> WITH
> OUR LADY
> OF
> FIFTH AVENUE

He stood and descended the stones. "Can you
excuse me, sir?" A few travelers ascended
the church's steps. "I don't mean to offend
you," he said through walls of shopping parades.
"You're not offending me," I said and waited.
I reached through the stream of the avenue
and put a dollar in his cup. "Thank you,"
he said. "You know I'm not a cheater

and I don't hurt nobody. I just need
a sandwich, so I'm asking folks to give
me change. See I'm a street person. I live
in the street. Only reason for that being
my wife kicked me out 'cause I caught her cheating
on me. I ain't going back. She was good
for a while, 'specially when we had food
and beer in the fridge. Man, I told that fucking
bitch that when I got a few more bucks in
change in my cup, I'd buy us a nice dinner—
wait a minute. Can I ask how you been
and if you have some liquor 'cause I might
have to fight the black folks later tonight.
You hear me call them that now, but I'll call
them the bad word later on. They're not all
bad, but sometimes you gotta do what's right.
I think maybe I want vodka tonight.
I go to the hospital when I'm broke,
but when there's money, I drink. I don't hocus
pocus. I tell it straight. I know you care,
so when you see those kids in Tompkins Square
Park asking for money, they ain't homeless:
they're living with mommy and daddy, dressed
in pre-ripped jeans from Sears, thinking they're hip
asking for change. I'd like to bust their lip.

Right in the kisser. Those fairies and queers
with their pierced bellies. You don't see 'em here
in the winter, do you? The weather turns
nice and suddenly they're homeless. Folks learn
from that and that's how come they don't give me
change—walk by thinking I'm one of those free
loaders. But I'm honest and I don't hurt
nobody. I might look a little dirty
'cause I ain't had a shower, but I do
alright for myself. Last night, took a few
sips of vodka, I admit, 'cause it's hot
in the daytime, but still it gets a lot
colder at night. Can't always find a church
or open train station. I used to search
downtown where I lived before I got fired;
my wife was cool back then, but she's a liar
and she was cheating on me, so I punched
her in the head. I gotta get some lunch,
maybe a Big Whopper with extra cheese—
now what the hell did I do with my keys?
What, you got somewhere to go? Well not me,
and if that asswipe pockets my money,
I'm gonna fight. I ain't a sissy. I'll
dropkick his fucking ass before he piles
up on me and robs me. As long as he

don't fuck with me, I don't hurt nobody."

6 Battle at the Wall

I left the narrator, heard him restart
the "change? change?" of his story,
and walked past shops *Located in the Heart*

of Manhattan, pigeon pecking concrete floor—
this world was a net, intersecting squares
and streets where workers hung on rungs

in the bottom of New York to fix the busted
city and riddle midtown tunnels' rusted
pipes, fiberglass faceguard striped with glare—

walked past dripping trucks, a broken
mouth, cracked sidewalks leading to subway stairs,
and you were my passport, my fire escape, directions

to a cliff—businessmen gathered—lights clicked
and they scattered past a parked van—"Don, is that ladder
buried?" "No, it's right here"—as smoke

rose from the world below. Walked the broken
city, crossed intersections, searching the grid
for traces of you—walked along brick

walls of churches, and everywhere
shadows of you—a voice in the cross,
eyes in the crowd, a streak of sunlit air,

past tables of burning incense and exhausted
travelers, and wherever you are, farewell,
my friend, and the road that was lost,

I send this note, that I'm on the way home
to a place once filled with shanties and stick ball
til Robert Moses, road-builder of New

York, destroyer of worlds, brought down old laws
and told Pharaoh, "Let my people through."
Traffic honked, a loose newspaper danced,

and this is how I will talk with you,
the rattle of a sidewalk grill,
rush of a cab, passing glance

from a stranger, these will be avenues
to you, and Annette, the room's still
on fire, the missed calls, a final kiss,

the last word I may speak to you is this—
boxes clicked and flashed   DONT
all across Manhattan—   WALK

passing cars barred the way to Central Park—
turned around, walked the same sidewalks,
through skyscrapered canal of 5th Avenue,

retracing same streets, everywhere the roar
of separation, casual shoes,
sales on winter coats—walked the broken side

walk of workmen in the same hole, exploring
insides of the same city—beside flipped
sewer lid, one half-emerged from the core,

orange helmet smeared with roots of New
York, and said, "Hey Larry, I need more light."
Walked along stone wall of Saint Thomas Church

where the man still sat. Put a dollar
in his cup. He stared at stone steps. Searched
his pockets. Didn't recognize

me. Returned to the street, crossed 53rd,
car honking like a diseased seagull. Air
conditioners dripped down dozens of floors,

splattering walkers and starring the stairless
sidewalk from cooler worlds above. Passed faces
searching skyline when the floor opened

and a man emerged from below—
the floor-door clanged shut beneath "Active Basement
Keep Clear"—and he pushed a truck cart through green

lights across the avenue. On the far shore,
saw a woman behind passing machines—
she divided in rush of flashing doors,

distorted through windows, reappeared
whole between cars before changing
again—and who was rearranged

in her eyes through clearings
in traffic and could almost see her eyes
when a car honked in a deranged birth cry.

Lights changed, a path cleared,
and we quietly passed as living ground
clicked its heels across 45th—

a distant siren and past the Chase
Manhattan Bank "change change" I heard
voices—"he wants to talk to me cuz he's feelin' me or
    whatever whatever and he's like 'cathy come to my crib'
    and I'm all about"
"change change"—
police car trapped in traffic, megaphone crackling,
"GO THROUGH THE LIGHT,"
driver hesitating before crossroads,
"GO THROUGH THE LIGHT"—
walked through wave of cold air
from shoe store, heard broken talk
"I never have rhythm I"
"go straight go straight you'll find"
change
        change
walked through crossroads,
waited for lights
to change
the core of living ground

change
        change
the strange
trails of side talks,
I need more light
and change
        change
don't be a stranger changing
my story tangled in your
change
        change
old laws hung on rungs
flashing doors to a cliff
to bust their lip
and change
        change
I left the narrator
I didn't mean it, I
change
        change
the floor opened
to let my people through
and I'm a stranger too
change
        change

faces from the underground
searching the grid for
change
        change
a man emerged from below
changed
        changed
cracked sidewalks leading to
a street person, I live in the street to
change
        change
where's 48th street
I need to unknot
I need to
change
        change
don't walk
chase Manhattan
and change
        change
open the door
and go through the light
and change
        change
brick walls of churches,

a broken mouth,
New York is all about
change
  change
open the floor
and open my eyes
and change
  change
I need more light
I never have rhythm I
change
  change
a broken world
smeared with roots of
change
  change
to fix the busted city
descending into the Earth to
change
  change
the bridge is falling
right in the kisser
Manhattan I Manhattan I
change
  change

7 Shape Shifter

I walked up Broadway, born before the grid,
    ancient war path of wooded Manahatta,
renegade cutting through the structured city,
    triangle maker of Times, Herald, Madison,
then squaring Union, and stealing away
    on a diagonal into the Battery—
        I walked uptown into the twilit blocks
            of a vanishing day,
last rays slipping into cloud as first splattering
    raindrops dotted the Upper West's sidewalks.

I walked uptown to meet Clarisse and arrived
    to find her clear umbrella's see-through borders.
"Stylish," I said. "The past has come alive.
    Looks like you're standing in film from the forties."
"This?" She twirled the umbrella. "This cost five
    bucks." "You see the world," I said, "and the world
can see you." She twisted her lips at me
and said, "I'll make faces at you. Shall we?"

    We walked through doors.
"How's the apartment search?" she said. Sat down.
"Met the cast of characters," I said. "Found

out the basic plot." Across polished floors
    waiters with trays
    danced their ballet
and swung plates to white cloth. "When did your flight
get in?" "David and I got back last night,"
she said. "We missed the fireworks." The restaurant dimmed
    its lights.

"It's good to get outside," I said, "to know
there's more to the world than Manhattan." "No,"
    she said. "Leaving this place,
you come to know there is no life outside
New York. I couldn't wait to get back. Fried
    calamari sounds tasty."

We sat by the window
in glow of street lamps, Broadway
streaming back and forth—
a candle shined between us—
bridge of light in a crossroad.

"I went for a wander," Clarisse said, "right
when we got back. I felt empty and wanted
to hear city sounds again, see the sights.
    I went for a wander

along Amsterdam and after I'd gone
ten blocks, sat on a wooden bench in bright
streetlights and watched walkers stop and move on,
the passing cars, and changing traffic lights.
The wood hurt my back, but I felt a bond
with it all. It's ages since the last night
      I went for a wander

alone. As I sat"—her voice made
the candlelight dance—"I was fading
away, deeper into the wood,
lights, and traffic. I was afraid

I'd disappear and quickly stood
up. My panic eased; it felt good
to walk again. And I remembered
walking a snowy neighborhood

along Broadway one warm December
night. The decorations resembled
little stars, steam rose from below,
but no cars passed, no subway tremors:

there was no sound. It felt as though
I was out of time, under glowing

ornaments with nowhere to go
but where I was: in steam and snow

and light." A waitress placed food by the circling
    candle-mist. "Thank you," I said. "That's a good
        story," I said to Clarisse. Steaming tea
and gloved waiters passed by. "Today at work,"
    Clarisse said, shaking salt over her food,
        "we were asking everyone, 'What would be
in people's heads, if you could see?' We said
    one guy had a circus tent and I would
        have an artist's studio inside me.
What would be going on inside your head?"
                "Let's see."

I thought a moment. "In my head,
there's a church being built,
but no sermonizing. Instead,
a band plays on the altar

making up songs with flutes, pianos,
and didgeridoos scattered
about so anyone can join
the band. And singers stuttering

scat lines and bebop at the pulpit
to whatever beat's playing.
Instead of rigid pews, floor pillows
are laid out. People dancing.

Those who'd rather not step to mic
sit because in this temple
everyone can do what they like.
Nobody pressures them

to dance or sing. They can just lurk
and listen if they choose.
Or they can even leave the church
if they don't like the music,

but it would be better if they
stepped to altar to sing,
picked up an instrument, and changed
the music to something

better, and in the door, foot traffic
of those uncertain, searching
for something else, and children laughing
'cause this is not a church

where people have to stop their voices.
And visitors amazed
at what's going on—and Clarisse
in the aisle making faces."

She caught herself smiling, stopped, and looked down.
    "That's not a church. It's a night club."
"It's both." She looked up and said, "There's this double
    sense to you I can't wrap my head around.
        It's like you're both ancient and new.
        Why is that?" "No idea. You
tell me." "It's like a different time shines through,
    but you're also very *now*, grounded
    here. You're from out of town,

yet it seems like you live here." She put cream
    in her coffee. "What in the world is 'didgeridoo?'"
"A wind instrument that sounds like a steam
    ship and played by Australian aborigines."
She smiled. "You played lots of Scrabble"—she stirred
the cream—"growing up?" "Why? What have you heard?"
    "You like to make stuff up. And play with words."

Broadway in the rain washed down the sidewalks
as the glass blurred traffic lights in uptown

crossroads. Clarisse told a story and found
herself in hallways long ago; she paused
at a room and turned, then her green eyes saw
a friend and blurred with tears. Traffic moved down
    Broadway in the rain.
"Clarisse—" I said. She started to withdraw
when I touched her hand. "It's fine. It's fine now."
Raised her hand to her mouth to stop the sound—
her eyes, wet streaks of green light, became Broadway
    blurring in the rain.

"You're not listening." "I am." "Where'd you go
    then?" "Your green eyes looked like Broadway," I said,
    "in the rain." She looked at me, her face red.
"See?" She dabbed her eyes with a napkin. "Shows
you make stuff up. Thank you." We sat enclosed
    in a long silence. "Tell me, if you're ready,
    of the painting you're working on," I said.
Her face lit up. "It's abstract. I don't know
if you'd like it." "Tell me." "It's a path hidden
    by colored splashes." We walked a yard filled
    with stone fences and flowers, turned a corner,
and as she talked, I saw an entire city
    in her face, a lifetime of streets and buildings.
    "It has threads, and shadows that look like doors."

There was a whole city behind her eyes—
I saw skylines and grafittied walls through
a world in her voice, streets in her replies,

as the first lightenings of a sunrise
streak the long corridors of avenues—
there was a whole city behind her eyes,

bridges to cliffs, metal spires scraping skies
in her stories, carts of flowers that grew
a world in her voice, streets in her replies—

silhouettes chalked into sidewalks—the horizon
flashed through buildings as she spoke and withdrew—
there was a whole city behind her eyes,

the real city revealed through the disguise
of her eyes, and camera shifts that renewed
a world in her voice, streets in her replies,

as if on the moon watching an Earthrise.
Candlelight shadowed her face from full view,
but there was a city behind her eyes,
a world in her voice, streets in her replies.

"Tell me a story,"
she said. "One that opens a door.
Tell me a story
I've never ever heard before
and reveals why you seem both new
and ancient. I like it when you
tell me a story."

"You want a story that's both old and new.
Let's see. Okay; think I've got one for you.

I'm in my house and the—" "*Your* house?" "My parent's
house. It's an ancient story. The lights go off and on
a few times. Then out. It feels like the air
is pulling away. My ears lock. I yawn,

but they stay locked, and then it happened. I
think I blacked out or maybe felt the strange,
sudden push through the house, but when my eyes
open and see again, everything's changed.

The roof is gone, the walls are gone, it's pouring
rain, and the house is busted into hundreds
of pieces, flying through the air, a roar
all around as if we've entered a tunnel

in another world, inside a sound we
don't understand. To my left is my sister.
Our mother—who we can hear, but can't see—
is to our right and lower down in this

collage of a house. I hear her voice say,
'Get down!' So I crouch down and see I'm kneeling
on her closet of winter coats and gray
scarves. My sister points down at the surreal

clothing and says, 'Mom!,' as if she were dead,
but I hear the voice say 'Get down!' above
the roar. Though it's not like tables or metal
things fly past so that we have to take cover.

It's more like the whole thing that used to be
the house is moving at the same speed, rumbling
through the air. As if the pieces aren't free
to scatter, but will remain linked in some

mysterious way. I find myself praying
to God, the same prayer again and again:
'Please God, help me. Please God, help me.' I say
this out loud into the chaos, suspended

in that other world, my voice the same volume
as the wind. My sister kneels on a door
in silence. Then the whole thing—busted walls
and all—lands. Not with a big thump, but more

with a sense that movement through air has stopped.
Unclear how long we flew or where we are.
It felt like a long time. My sister drops
from view and climbs down to whoever's yard

we've just landed in. My mother walks past
the hill of rubble. 'Let's go.' My leg pinned
under the TV, I sit in the blast
site, outside of time. It's no longer windy

and mostly calm, but the rain is still falling
hard. My mother's voice says again, 'Let's go!'
I free myself from the TV and crawl
down the twisted wood to the world below,

using windows and furniture as ladders
to the ground. The street is unrecognizable.
Left-side houses are gone; the right-side pattern
of houses remains. It's a war zone. I

can't see much, just dark, dark clouds pouring rain.
We walk the street and see other survivors
also walking toward the one house remaining—
shattered windows, but still there. We're alive

on the lawn in a daze. Knock with the brass
ring as if visiting for afternoon
tea. Look through windows at darkness. Click glass
panes. Nobody's home. The homeless and wounded

watch the house that shelters no one, a hollow
shell on an empty street. A woman turns
the door knob. 'Jeepers, it's locked,' she says. All
stare at the door at the end of the journey.

A woman asks someone to hold her baby
and, maybe eight months pregnant, heaves her shoulder
into the door. The house trembles. The neighbors
take a step back. She heaves again and molding

splits with a loud screech as the door unhinges
and falls in. We're amazed and step across
the fallen door, invade the house, continuing
through the hall and kitchen, past herbs and sauces,

into the living room. A dozen soaked
intruders sit around the coffee table.
The house whistles in wind. I look out. Broken
trees bow to the ground. Rain splatters panes. Cables

twist through branches. I say my second prayer
silently—*please God, let this house survive*—
while the others talk about a nightmare
and wait for ambulances to arrive

with help." We drank from cups like priests
at altar. "Was it," said Clarisse,
"a tornado?" "Grown-ups who knew
    all said so.
    I don't know.
        It was thunder
        and a tunnel
to another world." A breeze blew

through the open door—
sound of steel on steel in haze—
horse carriage galloped Broadway.

The candle had burned
itself out in the glass of melted wax.
"I think there's a reason you told me this story,"
Clarisse said.
"It's not just a tale from the past.
Maybe you can open yourself to the wind again,
see where you might fly to? See what happens
when the wind erases
the
world?"

Saturday, 6 July 1996

8 Flight from the City

I walked out of the city through the woods—
trees descended into the Earth, deep quiet
of the ground that silenced city sounds—hooded
stems, vine-hoops, flowers gathered in full riot.
Walked through smells of last night's rain, branches ringing
in on themselves, spinning into side-worlds.
Trees splashed into the air like fountains—springs
of jagged brush-line, swaying vine, leaf-curl.
I walked through the foliage, around the arced
planks of the theater, past the pond, and strolled
alone into the heart of Central Park.
A breeze danced through leaves and I felt that holy
    wind from long ago that blew my life here
        to these trees, this blesséd Earth, and Shakespeare.

Joined the line that had started long ago,
wound around trees, stretched along the pond. Sat
behind embroidered quilts spread out with rows
of wine bottles, cheeses, and card decks. Hatted
ladies fanned themselves beside wicker baskets;
boys with cut-offs kicked a hacky-sack high
in the air. A man stopped walking to ask,
"Is this a line of some sort?" "Shakespeare," I

said. "Oh. The tickets for the Shakespeare?" "Yes."
The line grew behind me, climbing a hill.
"Guys, I don't know the park that well"—"I guess
if you take everyone here, it would fill
    a theater." A man passed me: "Around here
    somewhere, I think, was cut-off point last year."

A man walked the line and said, "Get your summary
of Henry Five. Two dollars. All you need
to know on the play. Two dollars." A woman
in a black Staff vest walked, stopped next to me,
and said, "If you're this far back in the line,
your ticket chances are slim." Some stood, scattered;
others sat. She walked toward the theater signs
and said, "Stay, stay—people back there look bad.
Y'all look good." The field unwound tendrils, threading
anchors into the soil—the morning lifted
through branches, shining leaf-light through the meadow.
Sat on the grass and waited. Shadows shifted.
    The angle of light altered by degrees.
    A rush of wind italicized the trees.

"Nice breeze," my neighbor said. "A welcome break
from this heat," I said. "Do that again, God,"
he said, looking up at the sky. "We're baking
down here. You think we'll get tickets?" I nodded.
"There's a chance," I said. In the line ahead,
the Staff woman said, "Okay. That's it then.
Last one." "That's it," a ticketholder said,
"for *Henry the Fifth*. Better luck with *Henry
the Sixth*." Brown patches spotted the field, flickering
tree-light across pink smudges, dandelion
smears—squawk of distant birds. I stood up, ticketless,
and walked toward the woods as a passerby
    said, "He's acting in a nice little spot
        downtown for Shakespeare in the Parking Lot."

Trees opened umbrellas and stood like pillars,
a hushed theater waiting for the first scene.
I imagined, unlisted on the billing,
a company of players walk through greenery
and enter the stage. I stood with the groundlings
below to watch the ancient play and saw
worlds in ashes that once were bustling towns
and city streets, one moment in the dawn
before sawn to dust, and the players danced
the *árkhélógos*, the truth about

the beginning, across the stage. Advancing
armies entered Trojan walls, fires burned out,
    and iambic feet danced lines in the ruins.
    When Moses approached and called "Who are you?"

into the darkness, another voice called
back: "I am that iamb." Star-crossed meetings
where Jesus showed light on a road to Paul,
who translated into language, repeating
a written Mark, when the temple was razed,
who wove papyrus pages with Greek traces
of Aramaic sounds. Dante, amazed,
rediscovered himself in empty spaces
between worlds, and reborn faces who gazed
at Michelangelo's unfinished faces
saw their own death masks baking in the blazing
sun. Tibetan monks pinched sand grains to place
    in colored *mandalas*, opening doors,
    then swept a cosmic broom across the floor,

the vibrant links dissolving, the controlled
style of high art smeared into a child's sandbox.
Scholars pulled scrolls from labeled pigeonholes,
unfolding cities gone mad—Alexandria,
Seville, and Berlin—where insiders folded

fabric and feared strangers—loose threads, the strands
of the new cloth—and, power-mad, missed holy
inquiry into their own minds, who banned
counterpoint in history's *déjà vu*,
misgauging how harmonies form, who burned
every *Ulysses* that sailed into New
York Bay as smoldering pages kept turning,
    who worshipped fixed words of vanishing sages,
    an anomaly that named entire ages,

til a Cage sat at piano keys, listening,
then stood and walked offstage into eternal
silence. Waves rose, the sky gone, tempest twisting
wooden planks into new worlds and, returning
home, the house gone, the cat sat on the mat
at the celestial threshold, watching cities
of star-clusters rise from the void. Manhattan
emerged, dripping light, from the cosmic grid
as sages dissolved their forms and dispersed
through space, stars that imploded and flashed traces
of dust in corners of the universe,
who dreamed of time's sudden end and replacing
    lost worlds—Babylon, Rome, Constantinople—
    with the city of God, whose sonnets opened

at closing time, whose sand castles collapsed
into whirlpools of light, who felt the sea's
undertow pull through history's time-lapse
stories of spring and fall where every tea
leaf spelled death, and for every Henry's blade
that glittered battlefield glory, there followed
a light that appeared through the mist, a Lady
Macbeth walking a candle through the hollow
play, shining shades across the *dharma*-field—
the deep Earth absorbed our patterns. Winds blew
through the old castles, cracked stones, and pierced shields,
and still continents shifted and redrew
    shorelines, rivers carved unmovable rock,
    and oceans washed broken walls of apocalypse—

still trees descended toward the core and splashed
the air, healing the wounds of signs misread
and the tallest towers gone in a flash,
who flew over spider-webs of lights spreading
from cities toward darkness, whose twinkling stars
glowed and vanished in a blink, who awoke
to rust-colored dawns in a smoking, charred
town that rose again wall by wall, and broken
stones of pyramids grew into a sphinx,
and who built towers on ash-heaps and eyed

the world in an eye vanish in a wink,
whose biodegradable soul searched skies
    for escape, then merged with the land of birth,
    as cities blinked and flashed across the Earth.

9 The Immigrants Arrive

I stepped into
the elevator and ascended
to the roof—passed flowers blooming
in the night, walked to the railing, and I
stopped—

at the edge
of the cliff,
thousands of lights shined
in silence—
small, yellow squares glowed
in the darkness—
                sculptures
of light outlined the sky,
towers checkered with gold,
CitiCorp flashing and Empire State striped
in colored bands, camera flashes
sparkling along the watch tower,
the costly perches
of the world overlooking cross
streets below

I saw light-filled windows

into the heart of the grid
and inside
every square, someone was doing something:
a baby sitter heating up leftovers,
a doorman reading the *Times*

I looked down over the
edge and saw the streets
were made
of crosses—
lines of blurred circles
shined
        silently
as if all sounds had been sucked
out of the city—
cars slid across, cabs turned
without honking, people passed
without talking or
cursing, quietly
moving
through the dark

I held the railing along the
rooftop as a breeze blew across
the top of the city—

an apartment went dark,
another lit up, and hidden
in each light
a city walker waited inside
walls, ironing a suit,
eating in silence, sitting by a door,
and to the faces looking
out, I was another light
in a black rectangle
as we made each other's glow, lit
each other's night

we'd been drawn
to this city,
the corners vibrating
with music, cafés charged
with voices,
everything alive and bursting
through their shells,
coffee-stained pages,
paint-smeared
studios, a tangle
of snapped guitar strings

I looked at the citizens

alone in their rooms,
preparing in silence, waiting
for the dawn, a custodian
sweeping a corridor
in circuit-boards of light,
a homeless man on the staircase
of God

we'd been born before
the grid, before leases
and closing doors,
and had lived here
all our lives
in the one light
that shined through
all apartments

we were the immigrants
who'd left dead-end
streets, starving villages, raving kings
for something else

we were the restless, the unsatisfied,
wandering outskirts of small towns,
ready to drop everything and slip away

into the night
to enter highways,
board trains, and fly skyways

we were the outsiders, the maladjusted,
desperate enough to step off the familiar
pier into a mysterious boat
and sail rough
ocean for weeks, seasick, depressed,
all but given up in rising
waves, blinding fog,
and shifting clouds
to awake
one morning to see
a dot on the horizon,
a speck in the haze slowly
widening, shores of a new
world approaching, everyone
lined along the railing, sailing
into the bay to see
Manhattan rising
from the Atlantic like a lost
city, windows glittering
in morning sun as we bumped
waves toward Liberty, gripped railings

in the oncoming wind
from green-robed Athéne who held light
for every Odysseús sailing
into New York Bay
and said, "tell me a story"
to strangers
entering the harbor,
"open a door," as the city
made room, rewoven with new
arrivals, "a story
I've never heard before,"
as Manhattan's music shifted with changes
when strangers arrived,
when we arrived
home
again,
drawn like a magnet toward the once
only imagined
now
more real than the real
after traveling
for eons across rough
waters of our minds,
ancient continents,
the darkness of our lives,

to gather here
inside golden squares
in a city
of light

Sunday, 6 July 1996

10 One More Strange Island

honk
something wrong
sat up
strange
honk honk
i where
i who
no memory
what i was   unfamiliar
what was here
couldn't remember
what was i
wall   ceiling   wood
unfamiliar
what took place
never before
put on glasses
shapes more defined
identity missing
nothing came
nothing familiar
far wall drawn blinds
still nothing

what strange place this
enclosed space
what i was what was it

looked at clock 8:25
time   now
right now   not stretching black space
bed was sofa
vaguely familiar
yellow carpet   wooden chair
buildings beyond blinds
slowly realized city
started returning to world
joe   ellen   apartment
returning to the world
and then remembered Manhattan.
Manhattan at 8:25 in the morning.
a living room started to focus,
grew familiar from the night before.
continuity. here before.
i knew this world.

honking trucks continued,
squeaks and thunder of stops and starts
rising from streets far below—

sunlight through blinds hit
my eyes, i
pulled wide the curtain,
sat up and cleaned my glasses—looked
out at the long shadows
of a city morning,
delivery trucks arriving,
dog walkers walking—
it was up and running again

joe and ellen still asleep,
their baby deep asleep
in an ancient world—
there was a quiet here i didn't want
to disturb, walked
slowly to the bathroom and took off my clothes,
stepped from tiled floor
into the shower and turned
the water—it hit
and ran down
my body

i stood in the stream, the warm
spray, then stepped out
of the water, dripping

onto carpet, cleaned
the fogged mirror,
and got dressed.
opened the door
and clear air rushed in—
stepped into living room—
joe and ellen sat in silence,
heads down
over newspaper spread on the table

"good morning," joe said, looking up.
"hope it was alright that i took a shower," i said.
"of course."
we spoke quietly as if sound was fragile.
"i woke up this morning and didn't know where i was," i said. "or who i was or even what i was. it was strange."
"what?" joe said.
"any news?" i said quickly, gesturing toward the paper.
"New York's last warship left port. sailed under the verrazano. the city walls are unguarded."
"so what's the game plan for today?" ellen said.
"there's a place downtown i want to look at," i said. "they're having an open house at one."
i ate breakfast with the family, then thanked them goodbye and stepped across the threshold.

"have you thought about a share?" ellen said.
"that might be the way to go," i said and walked down the hall.

elevator dropped me down,
descending toward the
world, walked
through the lobby where the doorman ignored
me as i walked across waxed floors,
vacuumed carpet,
and opened the glass door—
it didn't feel right
til i stepped to the street and New York
dawned on me, gray buildings growing
out of gray sidewalk

the world had shaken loose,
become itself again—
walked over concrete squares,
metal grills, and turned
onto 53rd
where sidewalk stretched
toward horizon—
stopped by a staircase,
crowds emerging

from the Earth,
steps littered with cigarettes dropped
like bread crumbs
on entering the underworld—
a few bewildered, looked for signs—
i waited, no one stopped to ask,
the crowd cleared, and i walked on

turned downtown onto 3rd—
a man shouted "gary" into an intercom
and a door buzzed open

i was in the middle of the world,
smoke rising from the street,
a laundromat door held open
by a stack of *Village Voices*

looked through eyes
of passersby, eyes like doorways,
dark secrets, eyes like caged birds,
strangers walking sidewalks
exchanging glances, watching dances—
looked through the procession
of stupored, seen-it-all-before faces,
the weathered eyes of lived-in places,

the wondered look of first-time-in-New-York faces,
the lights of the city,
the long living sidewalks,
walking in our many-rhythmed paces
down the streets of New York

heard voices
of strangers in the mysteries
of the cross—
"first item of business is to slow down"
"sound like we were real out of towners"
"cultivating these leads and creating"
"New York with bad legs, you're always going up or down
    and all around"
to the gathering corners—
stopped at 33rd,
stepped to the curb,
and stood at the crossroads, waiting
for the world
to begin

lights changed and we were moving
again, doors of delis opening,
police car, siren singing,
as interweaving voices walked by

"mister smarty pants, let's see if"
"you love being in my business, it's amazing,"
"it's james thompson. a catalyst for change. got any?"

i put a dollar in the offering cup
and crossed 28th
toward flashing DONT WALK
that flashed on every block in Manhattan
past immigrants moving north,
women carrying yoga mats—
New York was alive in the arrival
of unfamiliar faces and
for one brief moment,
3rd ave was silent. heard
a voice across the street,
a bag brush against a light pole,
turning page of a magazine—
heard the world waking
from a long slumber,
then a single car drove past
as if from long ago
down an oddly empty street,
its tires brushing smooth pavement,
then a rush of cars filled
the avenue

waited at 14th when down
the block, a woman smiled
at a familiar face
in the distance, her smile growing
as she moved closer
as if ready to stop any one of us
and embrace the long-lost friend—
tried to spot the friend among the walkers,
thinking it's her, no it's him,
but she continued past stranger
after stranger, her smile growing,
then past me, and i turned
around to see the friend,
but she crossed 3rd ave and vanished
into Manhattan

i crossed 14th and stepped out
of the stream, stood
by the wall
as the crowd moved past and there i heard
the holy ones—
i lifted the lid and tuned in
for a listen
"'cause this is the shit, you know"
"you got some skills, i see you moving"

"money and the honey, so dig"
"your own damn lunch, 'scuse my language"
"bridge was a parking lot"
"of all the stupid things i go and"
"live in the low twenties, i can easily"
"surprised i don't see you on the subway"
"being all surface like hi how you doing"
"going from the sublime to"
"centre street and have to go in front of a judge and explain"
"i'm more of a small city person"
"looking for what's her face"
"who takes any little thing and blows up"
"fourteenth street is what the sign"
"lord came over and tiled the"
"rain and caddies drying him off, he's got"
"four beats and they all got rejected by"
"daht da-daht da-daa, this, that, and a third"
"got the nerve, right, to"
"tell me *some*thing—don't tell me everything"
"was an old piano, a box to bang"
"my way around the city, but there's just gaps and gaps of"
"miss goody two shoes over"
"name's mario, what's the scenario, you ladies"
"escaped because the british had no idea that"
"we don't eat flowers, alison, take those"

"left at twenty first and make sure to"
"slow down jeremy, oh for god's"
"came down with a bad case of mono"
"trying to get the story straight"
"for mister right and hey! small world—look who's"
"taking the train my whole life, right,"
"around the what cha mah call it"
"he gets all like baby"
"get fired, you'll get a week without"
"everyone cracking up, i was dying"
"to be born lucky; i was also born"
"good to get the face with the name"
"asleep on the train and woke up in"
"a beginning, middle, and end type of person"
"but there already were two goddesses, so i got a zebra hat"
"pregnant for joseph, all i could do was"
"send a fucking cop after this guy to"
"take a right on saint mark's and go down"
"on fire before the all star break, swinging"
"perfect english, everything, he can forget"
"me know when it's over, give me a"
"door guy acts like he can't see me"
"be all to end all or nothing, but"
"mary freaking sunshine wouldn't even"
"have italian in me, i have"

"no honey, we're not going to carry"
"no middle of the night people looking"
"to go on a wild goose chase"
"all up and down the thing a mah jig"
"it's just he said she said"
"by those people plugged in to"
"the battery, eat, and then we'll get"
"hi! been here long? i just got my nails"
"on your mark, get set, go"
"melt my horn down and make a ring"
"of New Yorkers do a lot of little"
"long story short, he caught me"
"making it up as they went a"
"walking, we're walking, come on, walk and talk"
"that bridge, it's like being in a different"
"wave 'cause it's two to one, three home"
"city has things, you know"
"that's so fucked up"
"that it becomes this urban"
"hello my good friend"
"Manhattan i"
"find a pair of boots and then i'm all done"
"doing test runs when"
"a minister, a rabbi, and the dalai lama walk into"
"a nice falafel on thompson, south of"

"nothing to worry about"
"and i was like what the? you know? and"
"i just gave someone really bad directions"

stepped back into the stream
across sidewalk and stopped—
waited for signs,
corners gathering
with strangers, lights changed,
and we walked a new
thread
into the grid

this street was a holy place,
intersecting voices, crosses
of languages
on the corner of 3rd
and everywhere

"hey stranger," said a man in the crowd.
we all turned—
we were all mysteries—

we turned again,
dancing along the grid,
and the morning spread
through spaces between buildings
as i walked down 3rd avenue
looking through New York eyes

Appendix: New Yorkers in "The Immigrants Embark"

1. Dante Alighieri, *Inferno* 18.79
2. Publius Vergilius Maro, *Aeneid* 1.438
3. Robert Frost, "Home Burial"
4. T. S. Eliot, "The Love Song of J. Alfred Prufrock"
5. James Joyce, *Ulysses* 13
6. Simon and Garfunkel, "The Sound of Silence"
7. Marcus Valerius Martialis, *Epigrammaton* 3.20.2
8. Oméros, *Odusseía* 15.401
9. Anonymous, "Lord Randal"
10. Walt Whitman, "Crossing Brooklyn Ferry"
11. Allen Ginsberg, "Mugging"
12. Walt Whitman, "Mannahatta"
13. Walt Whitman, "Crossing Brooklyn Ferry"
14. Anonymous, *Job* 1.7
15. Dante Alighieri, *Paradiso* 10.64
16. Aurelii Augustini, *de civitate Dei contra paganos* 1, *Praefatio*; Robert Frost, "Acquainted With the Night"
17. National Broadcasting Corporation, *Saturday Night Live*
18. Robert Frost, "Acquainted with the Night"
19. Józef Teodor Konrad Korzeniowski, *Heart of Darkness*

20. John Keats, "Ode to a Nightingale"
21. T. S. Eliot, "The Love Song of J. Alfred Prufrock"
22. Robert Frost, "Acquainted with the Night"
23. Walt Whitman, "Song of Prudence"
24. Emily Dickinson, "I felt a Funeral, in my Brain"
25. Edgar Allen Poe, "The Raven"
26. Derek Walcott, *Omeros* 9.3.30
27. Creedence Clearwater Revival, "Proud Mary"
28. Langston Hughes, "The Negro Speaks of Rivers"
29. Dante Alighieri, *Purgatorio* 10.139; William Shakespeare, *The Tragicall Historie of Hamlet, Prince of Denmarke* 5.2.309; William Shakespeare, *Antony and Cleopatra* 4.15.59; Gerard Manley Hopkins, "Not, I'll not, carrion comfort, Despair, not feast on thee"
30. Anonymous, "Lord Randal"
31. Publius Vergilius Maro, *Aeneida* 4.67
32. Franz Kafka, "Ein Landarzt"
33. Bobby Sharp, "Unchain My Heart"
34. Wallace Stevens, "The Emperor of Ice Cream"
35. Anonymous, "Westron Winde"
36. The Beatles, "The Ballad of John and Yoko" and Anonymous, "Westron Winde"
37. Anonymous, "Westron Winde"

38. Publius Vergilius Maro, *Aeneida* 4.595
39. Publius Vergilius Maro, *Aeneida* 4.595; William Shakespeare, *King Lear* 4.7.52
40. Publius Vergilius Maro, *Aeneida* 4.595
41. Robert Lowell, "Dolphin"
42. Walt Whitman, *Song of Myself* 3
43. W. B. Yeats, "Lapis Lazuli"
44. Wallace Stevens, "The Idea of Order at Key West"
45. Vyas, *Bhagavad-Gītā* 11.32
46. Walt Whitman, *Song of Myself* 26
47. Yehuda Amichai, "Jerusalem, 1967"
48. Friedrich Nietzsche, "Von alten und neuen Tafeln" 2, *Also Sprach Zarathustra* 3
49. Theodore Roethke, "I Knew a Woman"
50. John Berryman, *Dream Song* 140
51. Oméros, *Iliádos* 22.299
52. Robert Lowell, "Coleridge"
53. Publius Ovidius Naso, *Metamorphoseon* 9.272
54. Robert Lowell, "Robert Frost"
55. William Shakespeare, *Shake-speares Sonnets* 29
56. Oméros, *Iliádos* 21.607
57. William Blake, "The Garden of Love"
58. John Keats, "When I Have Fears that I May Cease to Be"

59. Marcus Tullius Cicero, *Pro A. Licinio Archia Poeta Oratio* 6.14
60. Dante Alighieri, *Paradiso* 30.132
61. Dante Alighieri, *Paradiso* 33.111
62. Dante Alighieri, *Inferno* 4.88
63. Tullius Laurea, "Perí Sapphò," *Anthologia Palatina* 7.17
64. Dante Alighieri, *Inferno* 7.47
65. The Replacements, "Here Comes a Regular"
66. Allen Ginsberg, "Kaddish"
67. John Berryman, *Dream Song* 219
68. The Alarm, "Spirit of '76"
69. Dante Alighieri, *Inferno* 2.32
70. T. S. Eliot, "The Love Song of J. Alfred Prufrock"
71. Mosheh, *Bere'shit* 23.4; Marcus Tullius Cicero, *de Oratore* 1.58.250; Paûlos, *Pros Ephesious* 2.19
72. Dante Alighieri, *Inferno* 23.126, *Purgatorio* 21.18
73. The Kinks, "Do It Again"
74. Oméros, *Iliádos* 21.608
75. Ioannes, *Apokalypsis Ioannou* 13.8, 20.15
76. Sylvia Plath, "Tulips"
77. Emily Dickinson, "I'm Nobody! Who are you?"
78. Oméros, *Odusseía* 9.366
79. Dante Alighieri, *Purgatorio* 7.7-8

80. John Donne, "A Valediction of my name, in the window"
81. Langston Hughes, "The Negro Speaks of Rivers"
82. Oméros, *Iliádos* 21.213
83. Pláto, *Politeia* 2.369 C
84. Anonymous, *Milindapañha*
85. Publius Vergilius Maro, *Aeneida* 3.161
86. Fyodor Dostoevsky, *Prestuplenie i Nakozanie* 5.4
87. Walt Whitman, *Song of Myself* 26
88. Dante Alighieri, *Inferno* 26.47
89. Paûlos, *Pros Korinthious* 1.15.51-52
90. Oméros, *Odusseía* 6.255
91. W. B. Yeats, "The Stare's Nest by My Window"
92. Oméros, *Iliádos* 21.361
93. Paûlos, *Pros Korinthious* 1.13.12
94. T. S. Eliot, *The Waste Land* 3
95. T. S. Eliot, "The Love Song of J. Alfred Prufrock"
96. Friedrich Nietzsche, "Die sieben Siegel (Oder: das Ja- und Amen-Lied)" 2, *Also Sprach Zarathustra* 3
97. Al Dubin and Harry Warren, "42nd Street"
98. W. B. Yeats, "The Mother of God"
99. Patrick Kavanagh, "Canal Bank Walk"
100. Robert Frost, "West-running Brook"
101. Talking Heads, "This Must Be the Place (Naïve Melody)"

102. Fyodor Dostoevsky, *Prestuplenie i Nakozanie* 2.1
103. Al-Qaeda operative, FBI wire tap, 2001
104. Matisyahu, "Warrior"
105. Alice Notley, *The Descent of Alette* 3
106. Alice Notley, *The Descent of Alette* 3
107. Gerard Manley Hopkins, "The Wreck of the Deutschland"
108. 'Til Tuesday, "Voices Carry"
109. Robert Frost, "The Lovely Shall Be Choosers"
110. Markos, *Katà Markon* 3.29; Loukas, *Katà Loukan* 12.10
111. Walt Whitman, *Song of Myself* 2
112. William Shakespeare, *Macbeth* 4.1.60-61
113. Fyodor Dostoevsky, *Idiot* 2.12
114. Loukas, *Katà Loukan* 14.21
115. Walt Whitman, "Give Me the Splendid Sun"
116. Publius Ovidius Naso, *Metamorphoseon* 7.645; T. S. Eliot, "The Love Song of J. Alfred Prufrock"
117. Muhammad, *As-Sâffât* 37.36
118. Publius Vergilius Maro, *Aeneida* 5.466
119. Taodue Film, *Francesco* 2
120. Theodore Roethke, "I Knew a Woman"
121. Publius Vergilius Maro, *Aeneida* 4.609
122. Dante Alighieri, *Purgatorio*, 12.77

123. Anonymous, *Śvetāśvatar Upanishad* 3.18
124. James Joyce, *Ulysses* 1
125. W. B. Yeats, "Adam's Curse"
126. Fyodor Dostoevsky, *Prestuplenie i Nakozanie* 6.8
127. James Blake and Charles Lawlor, "The Sidewalks of New York ('The Bowery')"
128. Vyas, *Mahabharat* 2
129. John Keats, "Ode to a Nightingale"
130. Ziggy Marley, "Higher Vibration"
131. William Shakespeare, *The Tragedy of Othello the Moor of Venice* 1.2.28
132. Talking Heads, "Road to Nowhere"
133. W. B. Yeats, "The Second Coming"
134. Valmiki, *Ramayan* 3
135. William Shakespeare, *Macbeth* 3.4.126
136. Pontius Pilate, *Katà Ioannen* 18.38
137. Anonymous, *Brihadāranyak Upanishad* 4.3.22
138. William Shakespeare, *Antony and Cleopatra* 4.15.84
139. Wallace Stevens, "The Snow Man"
140. Anonymous, *Beowülf* 1.9-10
141. William Shakespeare, *The Life of King Henry the Fifth* 4.1.251
142. William Carlos Williams, "Portrait of a Lady"

143. Osho, *Autobiography of a Spiritually Incorrect Mystic* 3
144. W. B. Yeats, "The Second Coming"
145. Robert Frost, "Mending Wall"
146. Michael Brandt, Derek Haas, and Chris Morgan, *Wanted*
147. Gerard Manley Hopkins, "The Wreck of the Deutschland"
148. Led Zeppelin, "Immigrant Song"
149. Yehuda Amichai, "Jerusalem, 1967"
150. D. H. Lawrence, "The Ship of Death"
151. J. R. R. Tolkien, "Roads go ever ever on," "The Last Stage," *The Hobbit*
152. Walt Whitman, *Song of Myself* 6
153. John Keats, "To Homer"
154. T. S. Eliot, "The Love Song of J. Alfred Prufrock"
155. Freakwater, "Great Potential"
156. Sundays, "Here's where the Story Ends"
157. William Shakespeare, *The First Part of King Henry the Fourth* 5.1.73
158. Gangaji, "Open End," *Hidden Treasure*
159. James Joyce, *Ulysses* 3
160. Anonymous, "Loki's Children and the Binding of Fenrir"
161. Walt Whitman, "A Noiseless Patient Spider"

162. Amiri Baraka, "A New Reality Is Better than a New Movie!;" Dire Straits, "Romeo and Juliet"
163. Haki Madhubuti, "a poem to compliment other poems"
164. Norah Jones, "Feelin' the Same Way"
165. William Shakespeare, *Romeo and Juliet* 4.3.41
166. W. B. Yeats, "The Circus Animals' Desertion"
167. William Shakespeare, *The Tragicall Historie of Hamlet, Prince of Denmarke* 2.2.540; Fyodor Dostoevsky, *Prestuplenie i Nakozanie* 5.5
168. W. B. Yeats, "Lapis Lazuli"
169. William Shakespeare, *Romeo and Juliet* 4.3.51
170. Quintus Horatius Flaccus, *Sermonum* 1.4.59
171. Fyodor Dostoevsky, *Idiot* 2.5; Anton Chekov, *Tri Sestry* 4
172. Robert Frost, Interview with Edward Lathem
173. Lao Tsu, *Tao Te Ching* 2, 10, 51
174. Walt Whitman, "Shut Not Your Doors"
175. Ioannes, *Apokalypsis Ioannou* 21.2
176. Mattaios, *Katà Mattaion* 25.35
177. Fyodor Dostoevsky, *Idiot* 2.3
178. Quintus Horatius Flaccus, *Sermonum* 1.4.58
179. Paûlos, *Pros Romaious* 11.19
180. Dante Alighieri, *Inferno* 18.79

181. Eric B. & Rakim, "I Know You Got Soul"
182. Matisyahu, "Chop 'Em Down"
183. Alice Notley, *The Descent of Alette* 2
184. Alice Notley, *The Descent of Alette* 2
185. Alice Notley, *The Descent of Alette* 2
186. William Shakespeare, *The Tragedy of Othello the Moor of Venice* 1.1.135-36
187. Walt Whitman, "Shut Not Your Doors"
188. Fyodor Dostoevsky, *Idiot* 2.2
189. Wallace Stevens, "The Snow Man"
190. Everly Brothers, "Bye Bye Love"
191. Sylvia Plath, "Tulips"
192. Jewel, "You Were Meant for Me"
193. Ioannes, *Apokalypsis Ioannou* 12.16
194. Malala Yousafzai, UN speech, 12 July 2013
195. Vyas, *Mahabharat* 1
196. Wallace Stevens, "Sunday Morning"
197. W. B. Yeats, "Byzantium"
198. Muhammad, *Al-An'âm* 6.129, *Jonah* 10.9, *Hûd* 11.17, *An-Nûr* 24.57, *Al-Hadîd* 57.15
199. Loukas, *Praxeis Apostolon* 18.25; Paûlos, *Pros Romaious* 12.11
200. Walt Whitman, *Song of Myself* 2

201. Osama bin Laden, Middle East Broadcasting Center, 17 April 2002
202. Apollonios Rhodios, *Argonautikon* 4.41
203. Lao Tsu, *Tao Te Ching* 1.9
204. Apollonios Rhodios, *Argonautikon* 4.42
205. Ricky Martin, "Living la vida loca"
206. Oméros, *Odusseía* 13.63
207. Hart Crane, "Cutty Sark"

Acknowledgements

I thank Vivian, who helped me get my first apartment in New York (no easy feat); Dave and Julie, who invited me to their high-rise apartment for a bird's-eye view of the city; and Jennifer, who showed me the coolest places in the East Village and Brooklyn.

I also thank all the people who have given feedback on the poem, including Dave, Gene, Peter, and particularly Carlos and Maria, as well as participants in various writing groups, particularly Jamie, who gave feedback on "Battle at the Wall" even after the group had disbanded.

And finally, I thank New York City, a magical place that turned out to be nothing like it first appeared.

About the Author

Erik Pihel is a poet and software engineer. He founded Palamedes Publishing, a creator of publishing software (www.ebookmaker.pub, www.responsivebooks.pub), and publisher of both printed and digital books (www.palamedes.pub). He has a PhD in English and a black belt in martial arts, and has been programming software for fifteen years.

www.ingramcontent.com/pod-product-compliance
Lightning Source LLC
Chambersburg PA
CBHW072057290426
44110CB00014B/1725